T0378310

GOAL

The Science Behind Soccer's Most Exciting Plays

by Eric Braun

CAPSTONE PRESS

a capstone imprint

Published by Capstone Press, an imprint of Capstone
1710 Roe Crest Drive, North Mankato, Minnesota 56003
capstonepub.com

Library of Congress Cataloging-in-Publication Data
Names: Braun, Eric, author. Title: Goal: the science behind soccer's most
exciting plays / Eric Braun.
Description: North Mankato, MN : Capstone Press, 2025.
Series: Sports illustrated kids: science behind the plays | Includes bibliographical
references and index.
Audience: Ages 8-11 | Audience: Grades 4-6
Summary: "Cristiano Ronaldo's brilliant overhead kick for Real Madrid. Alessia
Russo's back heel goal against Sweden. Gordon Banks's diving save that denied
Pelé. Diego Maradona's unreal goal in the World Cup. From forces of motion to
the transfer of energy, science plays a huge role in these big moments.
Examine each part of these unforgettable plays and find out how science
makes them happen"—Provided by publisher.
Identifiers: LCCN 2024032646 (print) | LCCN 2024032647 (ebook) | ISBN
9781669091929 (hardcover) | ISBN 9781669092193 (paperback) | ISBN
9781669091967 (pdf) | ISBN 9781669092209 (epub) | ISBN 9781669092216
(kindle edition)
Subjects: LCSH: Soccer—Juvenile literature. | Science—Juvenile literature.
Soccer players—Juvenile literature. Classification: LCC GV943.25 .B72 2025
(print)
LCC GV943.25 (ebook) | DDC 796.33409—dc23/eng/20240716
LC record available at https://lccn.loc.gov/2024032646
LC ebook record available at https://lccn.loc.gov/2024032647

Editorial Credits
Editor: Christianne Jones; Designer: Jaime Willems; Media Researcher:
Svetlana Zhurkin; Production Specialist: Whitney Schaefer

Image Credits
Getty Images: AFP/Staff, 27, 28, Archivo El Grafico, 25, 29, Dave Howarth–
CameraSport, 16, Emilio Andreoli, 9, 10, GeorgiosArt, 8 (Newton), Hulton
Archive, 17, Naomi Baker, cover (left), 1, 13, 15, Popperfoto, cover (right), 21,
22, 23, Popperfoto/Rolls Press, 19, Real Madrid/Angel Martinez, 7; Newscom:
Cal Sport Media/Jonathan Moscrop, 14, Zuma Press/Massimiliano Ferraro,
11; Shutterstock: Alex Kravtsov, 5, Alex Macrovector, 20, Deviney Designs
(powder), cover and throughout, lumyai l sweet, 9 (referee), Marina Sun (math
background), cover and throughout, Vector Tradition (soccer ball), back cover
and throughout

Printed and bound in the USA. PO 6121

TABLE OF CONTENTS

Words in **BOLD** are in the glossary.

SCIENCE AND SOCCER

Soccer has a long history of dazzling fans. Professional soccer was first played in England in the mid-1800s. However, a version of the game was played in China long before that. The game has changed since then, but the incredible skills and amazing plays still feel like magic.

But those plays are not magic. They are science mixed with skill. A player kicks the ball, and unseen **forces** come alive. The ball flies through the air, propelled by the power of the kick. It is affected by other forces, such as **gravity**. With every touch, **energy** is exchanged.

Let's explore how science affected some of the most exciting plays in soccer history.

CHAPTER ONE

DEFYING GRAVITY

Cristiano Ronaldo is one of the greatest soccer players of all time. He has scored more goals in professional play than anyone else. Perhaps the most impressive goal took place on April 3, 2018.

Ronaldo was playing for Real Madrid. It was the quarterfinal of the Union of European Football Associations (UEFA) Champions League against Juventus of Italy. Ronaldo passed to Lucas Vázquez, who fired a shot on goal. The goalie deflected the ball back into play. As Dani Carvajal of Real Madrid took control of the ball, Ronaldo moved in front of the goal.

FACT

Ronaldo's goal was so spectacular that even the opposing fans stood up and cheered.

Ronaldo kicked as he flipped to score a stunning goal.

Carvajal sent a high pass his way. Ronaldo was facing away from the goal as he leaped into the air. He flipped upside down and nailed a perfectly timed kick. How is that possible? Forces and **motion**! Let's look to scientist Isaac Newton for further explanation.

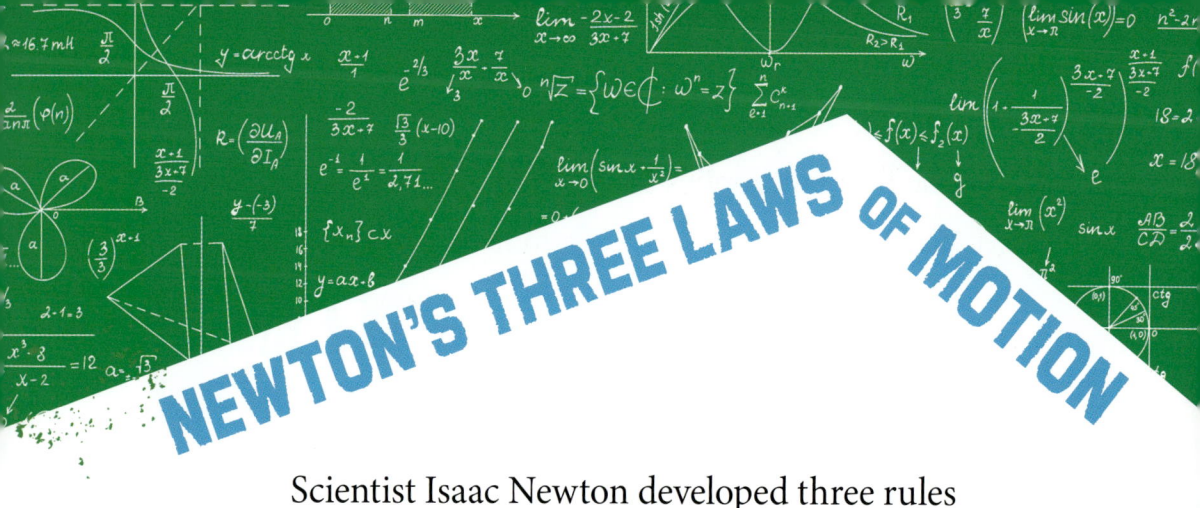

NEWTON'S THREE LAWS OF MOTION

Scientist Isaac Newton developed three rules about motion. These are known as Newton's laws of motion, and they play a huge role in every game.

1. An object remains at rest or in motion until it's affected by a force.

2. The greater the mass of an object, the more force it will take to move it. In other words, force equals mass times acceleration (F = ma).

3. For every action, there is an equal and opposite reaction.

The first law applies to Ronaldo's jaw-dropping play. An object remains at rest or in motion until it's affected by a force. A force is a push or a pull. Gravity is a force. It pulls on us and holds us to the ground.

Ronaldo was bound to Earth by gravity. So how did he jump so high into the air? He created his own force using his powerful legs. When two forces work against each other, the stronger force wins. Ronaldo's force was much stronger than gravity.

Ronaldo timed his jump perfectly to meet the ball in the air.

When Ronaldo's foot connected with the ball, it was almost at the height of the crossbar.

Science also tells us that an object's motion provides **evidence** to **predict** its future motion. Ronaldo noticed the ball's speed and height. He predicted exactly when to jump. His timing was perfect. He kicked the ball cleanly at the peak of his jump. With his swinging leg, Ronaldo applied a new force to the ball. This changed the motion of the ball.

There was no way for the goalie to stop Ronaldo's magical shot.

Ronaldo's shot whizzed past the stunned goalie and into the corner of the net. GOAL!

BIKING UPSIDE DOWN

When a player leaps into the air, somersaults backward, and kicks a ball behind him, it is known as a bicycle kick. This thrilling kick gets its name from the motion of the legs, which makes it look like the player is pedaling a bike—upside down, of course.

CHAPTER TWO

THE BACK HEEL BOOT

It was the UEFA Women's Euro 2022 semifinal. England led Sweden 2–0 in the second half of the game. To ice the win, the English played a slow and steady game. But that didn't mean they wouldn't try to score again if they had the chance.

They sensed such a chance in front of Sweden's goal. Keira Walsh made a pass to Fran Kirby. Kirby sent it to striker Alessia Russo. She was full of **potential energy** and in great position to shoot.

Russo used motion and energy to take the ball down the field.

potential energy: stored energy

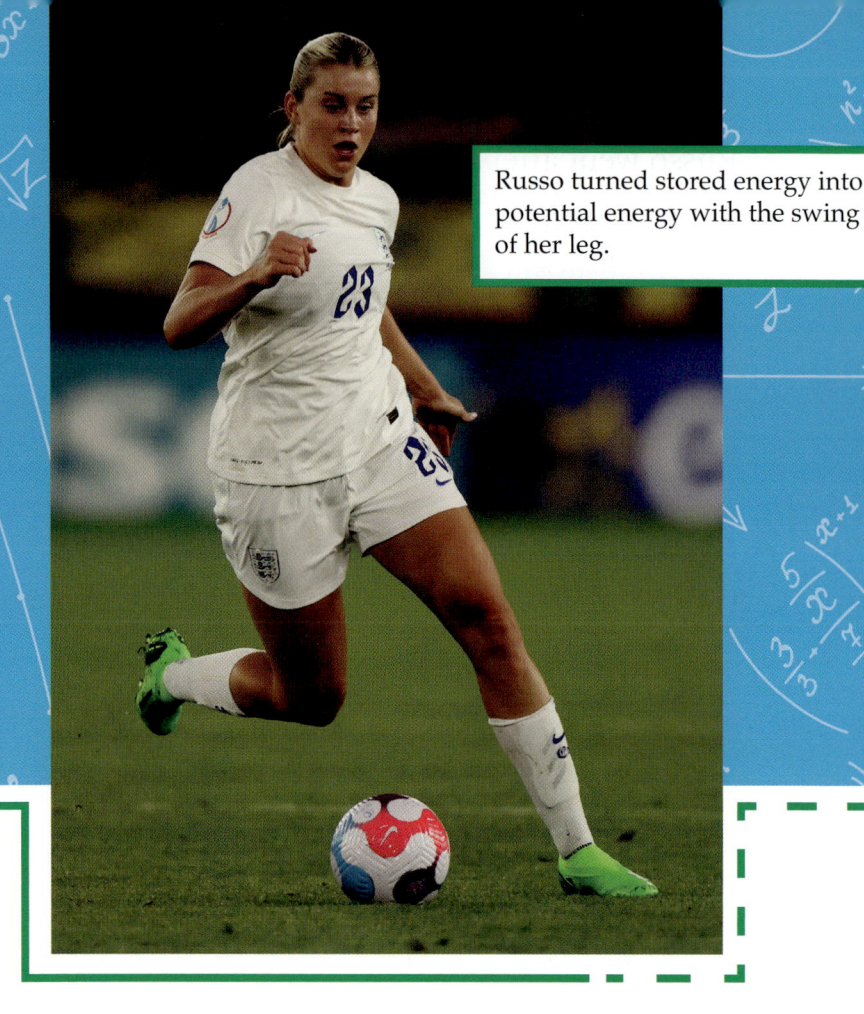

Russo turned stored energy into potential energy with the swing of her leg.

Russo extended her right foot back while planting her left foot. Her cleats dug into the ground, providing **friction**. She used the energy of motion, or **kinetic energy**, to swing her right foot forward. This was her way of creating a force that pushed the ball forward. The shot was fierce, but the Swedish goalie deflected it. The ball rolled away from the net.

Russo went after it, a Sweden defender on each side. At this moment, the ball, Russo, and the two defenders were in motion away from the goal. That's a lot of motion going in the wrong direction.

The expected way for Russo to change the ball's motion would be to first change her own motion. Then she could attack the ball face on. But her movement was limited by the two defenders. What could she do?

Russo beat the defenders to the ball and worked for control.

Russo bumped one defender with her shoulder, gaining some space. But the other defender was still cutting off her chance to turn toward the goal. Russo didn't want to lose momentum or the ball. So she applied a new force to the ball with her heel.

Without turning around, Russo swung her foot over the ball and knocked it backward with her heel, right past the surprised goalie. GOAL!

Russo kept her momentum and used it for an epic heel kick.

THE BRITISH LADIES FOOTBALL CLUB

In 1895, Nettie Honeyball created the British Ladies Football Club. It was the first known women's professional soccer league. They faced criticism, violence, and threats from people who didn't think women should play a "man's sport." The league ended because it became unsafe to play.

CHAPTER THREE

THE BIG DENIAL

It's been called the greatest save in the history of soccer. It happened in a match between two power-house teams at the 1970 World Cup. England was the defending champion. Brazil had won the two cups before that.

The game also involved two of the world's biggest soccer stars. Brazil's Pelé was at the height of his career. He was a worldwide superstar. England's Gordon Banks was an accomplished goalie. He was named Fédération Internationale de Football Association (FIFA) goalkeeper of the year six times.

The game was a tight, defensive battle. Following a shot on goal by England, Brazil sent the ball up the right side. Brazil winger Jairzinho raced after it.

Goalie Gordon Banks (navy jersey) lined up with his team before the 1970 World Cup.

At this point, the ball was rolling very quickly—much quicker than Jairzinho could run. As we know from Newton's first law, an object stays in motion unless acted on by another force. Luckily for Jairzinho, other forces were acting on the ball as well. One force was gravity, which was pulling the ball downward. This slowed the ball by creating **resistance** against the grass.

Another force was the air surrounding the ball. Even though we can't see air, it is not *nothing*. It's made up of **molecules**, just like everything in the world. And those molecules push back on a moving object. That force also slows the ball.

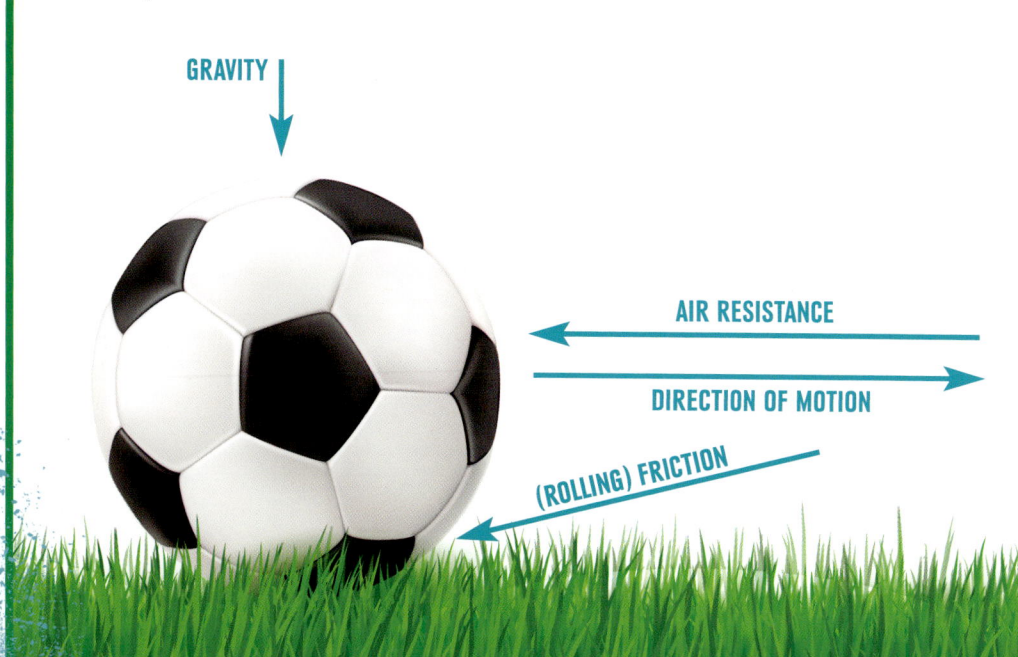

GRAVITY

AIR RESISTANCE

DIRECTION OF MOTION

(ROLLING) FRICTION

Those two forces caused the ball to slow down. However, Jairzinho did *not* slow down. He kept running at full speed. He caught up to the ball at the end line and sent it to the far side of the penalty box.

Using speed and energy, Jairzinho beat a defender to the ball.

Pelé (far right) watched as the ball headed toward the goal.

Banks was at the post by Jairzinho, anticipating a shot. When the pass whizzed to the far side, Banks was suddenly out of position. Pelé was there to receive the pass. He jumped high into the air and knocked the ball down with his head.

According to Newton's third law of motion, when one object exerts a force on another object, the second object exerts an equal and opposite force on the first. Pelé applied a force to the ball with his forehead, and the ball changed direction.

A moving object contains energy. The faster it's moving, the more energy it has. Some of the ball's energy went into Pelé's head and body. That energy forced him to take several steps back when he landed on the ground.

The ball went down toward the turf in front of the net. Pelé had put it exactly where he wanted it. It would bounce off the grass and into the net—a sure goal. In fact, he began celebrating before he realized a diving Banks had deflected the shot. No goal!

The ball bounced wide of the goal after an incredible save by Banks.

FACT

Even Pelé was impressed by the save. He later said, "I couldn't believe what I saw . . . I can't believe how he moved so far, so fast."

CHAPTER FOUR

CONTROVERSY AND GREATNESS

The 1986 match between Argentina and England featured one of the most controversial goals in World Cup history. It also featured one of the greatest goals in World Cup history. Argentina's superstar Diego Maradona was at the center of both of them.

Let's start with the controversial goal. Maradona leaped to head a ball into the goal. Instead, he hit it with his fist. That is a rules violation, but the referees didn't see it. The ball sailed into the net and was counted as a goal. Maradona and his teammates celebrated while the England players complained.

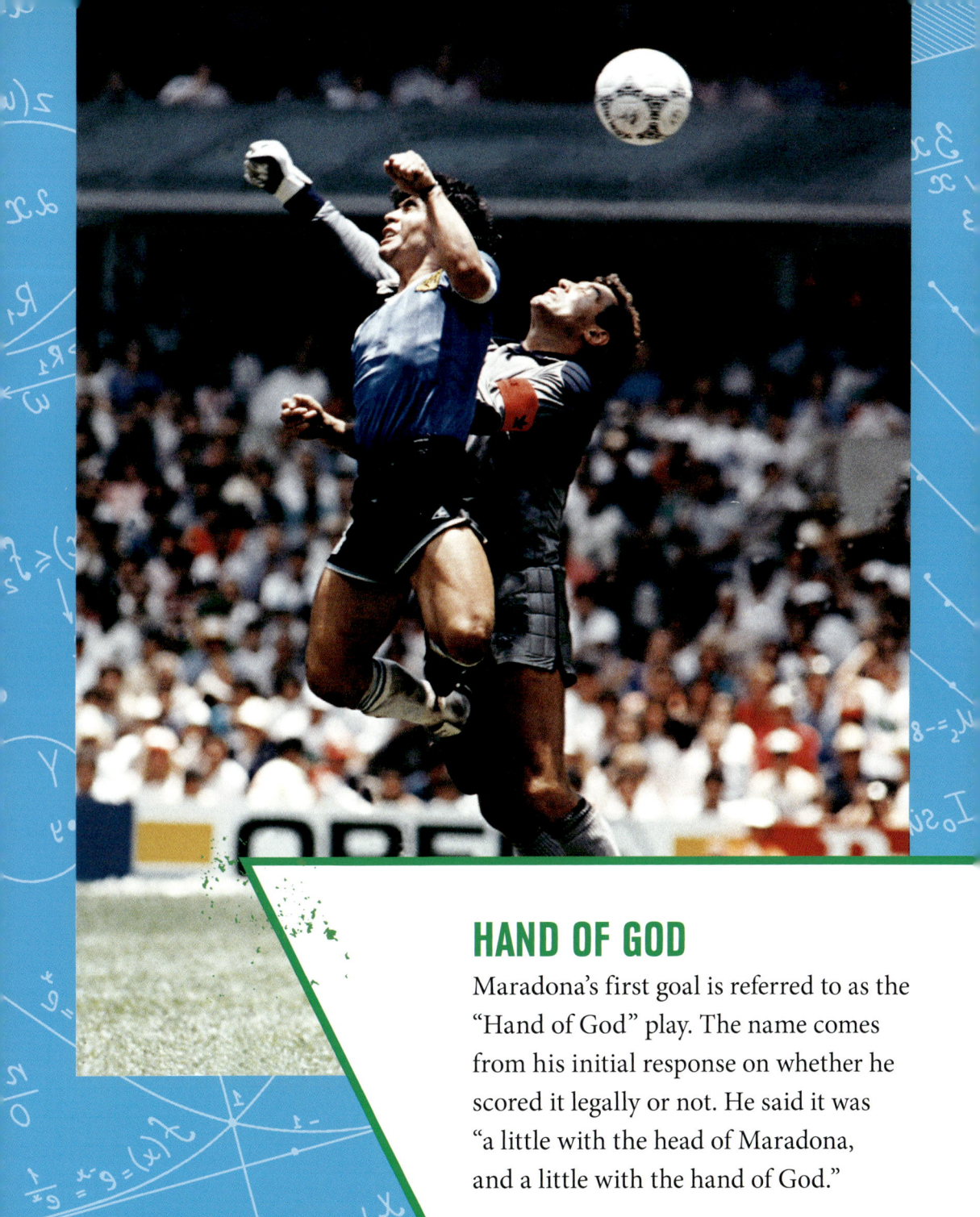

HAND OF GOD

Maradona's first goal is referred to as the "Hand of God" play. The name comes from his initial response on whether he scored it legally or not. He said it was "a little with the head of Maradona, and a little with the hand of God."

There would be no controversy about Maradona's next goal. Maradona received the ball deep in Argentina's side of the field, stopping a swift pass from a teammate. The ball carried energy from the force applied by the passer. Maradona stopped it by applying his own force. The trick was to apply just the right amount. If he applied too much force and energy, the ball would bounce back the other way.

Two defenders were already pouncing on him. But Maradona controlled his force and energy. He quickly moved the ball toward his own goal. He burned by four more defenders.

Many forces were acting on the ball as it rolled along with Maradona. The graceful nudges and taps from Maradona's feet. The gravity pulling the ball downward. The resistance from the grass. These forces slowed the ball and helped Maradona predict how it would react to his movements.

FACT

Maradona touched the ball 11 times in his 11-second dash. Each touch was the perfect application of force to alter the ball's motion away from a defender and closer to England's net.

The goalie dove to the right, completely tricked by Maradona's movements.

Maradona drew near the goal on the right side. The goalie positioned himself to close off Maradona's angle to shoot. An object's motion can be used to predict its future motion. The motion of Maradona and the ball was headed directly toward the goal.

The goalie predicted their motion would continue straight on. To stop a potential shot, he stepped up to attack. But Maradona faked the goalie by touching the ball one more time, dragging it farther to the right side.

Maradona taps the ball into the net to score his legendary "goal of the century."

Because the goalie had moved to his right predicting the ball's new direction, Maradona had a clear shot. He just needed one last tap on the ball to roll it in. GOAL!

Soccer is known as the beautiful game. The talented players and elite skills are legendary. And with science working behind the scenes every step—and kick—of the way, it will continue to amaze fans forever.

GLOSSARY

energy (EH-nuhr-jee)—the ability to do work

evidence (EH-vuh-duhns)—information, items, and facts that help prove something to be true or false

force (FOHRS)—an action that changes or maintains the motion of a body or object

friction (FRIK-shuhn)—a force that slows down or stops motion between two things that are in contact

gravity (GRAH-vuh-tee)—an invisible force that pulls objects toward each other; Earth's gravity pulls objects toward the ground

kinetic energy (kuh-NEH-tik EH-nuhr-jee)—the energy of motion

molecule (MAH-luh-kyool)—the smallest unit of a substance, containing one or more atoms

motion (MOH-shuhn)— the act of moving or having momentum

potential energy (puh-TEN-shuhl EH-nuhr-jee)—stored energy

predict (prih-DIKT)—to figure out in advance what will happen

resistance (rih-ZIH-stuhns)—an opposing or slowing force

READ MORE

Baker, Laura. *Physics for Curious Kids: An Illustrated Introduction to Energy, Matter, Forces, and Our Universe!* London, England: Arcturus Publishing, 2022.

Troupe, Thomas Kingsley. *Strikers and Scarves: Behind the Scenes of Match Day Soccer.* North Mankato, MN: Capstone, 2023.

Turner, Myra Faye. *Discovering Forces and Motion in Max Axiom's Lab.* North Mankato, MN: Capstone, 2025.

INTERNET SITES

American Museum of Natural History: OLogy | Physics
amnh.org/explore/ology/physics

Ducksters: Physics for Kids
ducksters.com/science/physics

KiwiCo: Soccer Science
kiwico.com/blog/the-science-behind/soccer-science

INDEX

ABOUT THE AUTHOR

Eric Braun is a children's author and editor. He has written dozens of books on many topics, and one of his books was read by an astronaut on the International Space Station for kids on Earth to watch. Eric lives in Minneapolis with his wife, two kids, and a dog that is afraid of cardboard.